NO BLUNDER DOWN UNDER

acacia press

Published by Acacia Press
PO Box 388 Corinda Brisbane Qld 4075 Australia
Ph 07 3716 0104 Fax 07 3716 0105
www.acaciapress.com.au

Copyright © 2011 Acacia Press
Reprinted 2012
Reprinted 2013

ISBN 978 0 9805839 5 3

Compiling by Robert Brown, Sue Tester, Selena Webber
Art and Design by Selena Webber

Produced by Jade Productions

NO BLUNDER DOWN UNDER

Australian slang utilises humour, wit, rhymes, bizarre experiences from the bush to the beach, familiar and personal to portray how experiences shape language and identity. For example, *'have a burl'* at something is similar to *'have a crack'*, and both phrases reflect a history of Australian improvisation and hard work as part of working in the bush.

Please note that some of the words and expressions in **No Blunder Down Under** may cause offence. It is not recommended to use such words and expressions, but they have been included as **No Blunder Down Under** is a book about the use of language whether it be good or bad.

A1   first class
ABC   Australian Broadcasting Corporation or Aunty
AC DC   bisexual
AFL   Australian football league
AO   adults only
APC   hand-wash arm pits and crotch
A big deal   important, serious
A bit much   rude, excessive
A bit rich   over-priced
A okay   very good
A over t/Arse over tit   falling over, stumbling
A real shit   a horrible person
Above board   legal
Abso-bloody-lutely   positively yes
Ace   the best, very good
Act the goat   foolish behaviour
Adams ale   water
Aerial ping pong   Australian Rules Football
Aggro   aggressive behaviour
Aggy pipe   terracotta drainage pipe
Akubra   a wide-brimmed hat
Al Capone   telephone
Alice, the   Alice Springs
Alko   an alcoholic, heavy drinker
All ears   listening attentively
All piss and wind   insincere, boastful
All rounder   good at many tasks or sports
All smiles   happy
All systems go   ready
Alrighty   okay, yes

Akubra is a popular brand of **Aussie** fur felt hats. The wide brim is a typical part of **Ozzie** culture.

Always in the shit   always in trouble
Always on the go   always busy
Amber fluid   beer
Ambo   ambulance
Ammo   ammunition
Amp   1. amplifier; 2. get excited
Anal   1. fussy, perfectionist, neat; 2. obsessive
Ankle biter   infant or young child
ANZAC   Australian and New Zealand Army Corps
Anchors   car brakes
Ant's pants   very good
Ape shit   raving mad
Apple Isle   Tasmania
Apples, she'll be   it'll be all right
Argue the toss   disagree
Argy bargy   an argument
Around the bend   crazy, mad
Arse end   worst part, tail end
Arse into gear   get going, moving, start
Arse off   depart
Arsey   very lucky
Arthur or Martha   a state of confusion
Arvo   afternoon
As crook as a dog   very unwell
As if   expression of complete disagreement, disbelief
As pissed as a newt   very drunk
As rough as guts   1. poor workmanship, rough; 2. uncouth person
As the crow flies   travel in a direct line
At death's door   dying, seriously ill
At full tilt   at full speed

ANZAC Day, 25th April is an important national occasion. It marks the anniversary of the first major military action fought by Australian and New Zealand forces in the Battle of Gallipoli during the First World War. The soldiers became known as **ANZACs**.

At odds   disagreement
At the crack of dawn   daybreak
At the drop of a hat   immediately
At the wheel   in control, in charge
Atta boy   approval
Aussie/Ozzie   an Australian person
Aussie battler   a working class person
Aussie rules   Australian football
Aussie salute   brushing away flies with your hand
'Ave a go   do something, get started
Avos   avocados
Awesome   1. excellent; 2. high quality
Axe/Axed   dismissed, get the sack
BBQ   barbeque
BYO   1. bring your own alcohol; 2. unlicensed restaurant
Back down   retreat from an argument
Back of beyond   a remote area
Back of Bourke   remote outback area
Backhander   hit with the back of the hand
Bad mouth   criticise unfavourably
Bad trot   period of misfortunes and bad luck
Bag   1. claim first; 2. unattractive woman
Bag of fruit   a suit
Bail out   to depart, leave a situation
Bail up   to physically corner somebody
Ball and chain   wife
Balmain bug   crab or crustacean
Banana bender   a Queenslander
Banged up   pregnant
Banjo   1. frying pan; 2. a shovel

Barbie   barbeque

Banker   a river or stream in flood

Barney   an argument or fight

Barra   fish called a Barramundi

Barrack   to cheer on a sporting team

Bash   1. attempt; 2. party; 3. assault someone

Batch   living on one's own

Bathers   swimming costume

Battler   one who struggles in life

Beanie   knitted brimless cap

Beaut/beauty   fantastic, excellent

Bee's knees   great, fantastic

Beer belly   beer drinking paunch

Belly-ache   to complain

Belly-button   navel

Bellyful   too much of anything

Belt   1. move quickly; 2. hit

Bender   drinking binge

Bend the elbow   a heavy drinker

Betcha   I bet you

Better half   wife

Bevan   lout, hooligan

Bewdie   1. beautiful, good; 2. approval

Bible basher   a religious person

Biddie   old woman

Bikkie   biscuit

Big girl's blouse   1. effeminate male; 2. timid

Big red   male red kangaroo

Big smoke   a big city, usually a capital city

Big spit   vomit

Rock on over for a **barbie** Saturday **arvo**. There'll be **heaps** of **snags**, **prawns** and **chook**. **BYO, down a few coldies** and **veg out**.

Big-note oneself   to boast or brag about oneself
Billabong   a waterhole
Billycan (billy)   a metal container to brew tea over the campfire
Billycart   homemade cart steered by ropes
Bin   garbage can
Bindi   plant with prickly seeds
Bingle   a minor car crash
Birthday suit   naked
Bite ya bum   be quiet, shut up
Bitser   an animal or person of mixed blood
Bizzo   doing business
Black stump, beyond the   long distance away
Blind   very drunk person
Blind Freddie   an unperceptive person
Blob   1. a fat person; 2. cricket score; out with no runs
Blockie   drive around the block
Bloke   a male person, fellow, chap
Blood house   a disorderly public house with a reputation for violence
Blood nut   a person with red hair
Bloody   very (the great Australian adjective)
Bloody galah   a silly person
Bloody oath!   I agree
Blotto   very drunk person
Blow   1. have a rest; 2. fail in something
Blow in   an uninvited person, stranger
Blow in the bag   breathalyser test
Blow me down   expression of surprise
Blower   a telephone
Blowie   a blowfly
Bludge   impose on one's generosity

Blowies are large, metallic coloured flies that lay their eggs on carcasses and other organic matter.

Bludger   a very lazy person
Blue   a fight
Blue-arsed fly   a blue blowfly
Blue heeler   an Australian cattle dog
Blue, make a   make a mistake
Bluey   1. swag; 2. traffic ticket; 3. redhead
Bluey   4. blue cattle dog; 5. bluebottle jellyfish
Blue flyer   female red kangaroo
Blunder   a mistake
Boardies   board shorts
Bobby dazzler   something very good
Bob's your uncle   all is well
Bodgy   false, worthless
Bog   going to the toilet
Bog house   outside toilet
Bog in   eat heartily
Bogan   loutish person
Bogged   vehicle stuck in the sand or mud
Boiler   an old woman
Bomb   1. run-down car; 2. make a large splash when jumping into a pool
Bomb   3. fail a test; 4. something very cool; 5. spray with graffiti
Boney   very thin, emaciated
Bonkers   out of control, crazy
Bonnet   car's front engine cover, hood
Bonzer   excellent, good
Boogie board   small surfboard, body board
Bookie   a bookmaker
Boomer   a large kangaroo
Boomerang   an Aboriginal weapon
Boot   car rear luggage compartment, trunk

The **bog house**, **dunny** or **thunder box** was found in most **Aussie** backyards until the mid 20th Century.

Booze   alcoholic drink
Booze bus   vehicle used for assessing a driver's blood alcohol concentration
Boozer   1. a pub or hotel; 2. a person who is a heavy drinker
Bored shitless   extremely bored
Boss cocky   an employer
Bottle shop   liquor store
Bottle-o   liquor store, bottle shop
Bottler   excellent!
Bottling, your blood's worth   a compliment of very special praise
Bouncer   a person employed to evict troublemakers
Bower bird   a collector of trash and many objects
Bozo   idiot
Brass   money, cash
Brass monkey, freeze the balls off a   very cold
Brass razoo, he hasn't got a   he is very poor
Breaker   a person who breaks in horses
Brekkie   breakfast
Brickie   a brick layer
Bring a plate   bring a plate of food to a party or barbeque
Brisvegas   Brisbane, state capital of Queensland
Brizzie   Brisbane, state capital of Queensland
Broke   no money
Brown eye   expose one's anus or bum
Brown nose   suck up to the boss, crawler, boot licker
Brumby   wild Australian horse
Bub   1. baby; 2. affectionate name for one's girlfriend or wife
Buck's night   stag party, male gathering on the eve before a wedding
Buckley's/Buckley's chance   no chance at all
Buddy   mate, pal
Budgie   budgerigar

Budgie smugglers   men's bathing costume
Bugger   1. person; 2. annoying person, nuisance; 3. cause inconvenience
Bugger all   very little amount
Bugger off   go away
Buggered   1. broken; 2. very tired
Built   good physique, well built
Built like a brick shit house   solidly built
Bull bar   a bar fixed to a vehicle to protect it against hitting wildlife
Bull dust   a lie
Bull shit   unbelievable statement
Bum   1. buttocks; 2. tramp; 3. get for nothing; 4. mild annoyance
Bum fluff   facial hair growth on a teenage male
Bum nuts   eggs
Bum steer   false information
Bundy   Bundaberg, Queensland and the rum that is produced there
Bung   1. damaged, broken; 2. place or put without care; 3. stopper
Bunyip   a mythical creature
Burl   try something
Burn   drive at high speed
Bush   rural Australia
Bush bash   to travel off road in a vehicle
Bushie   a person from the bush
Bushranger   an outlaw
Bush telegraph   gossip network
Bush whacker   a derogatory term for a person from the outback
Butcher   a small glass of beer in South Australia
Butcher's hook   cook or chef
By jingoes   exclamation of wonder
Cab sav   cabernet sauvignon wine
Cabbie   taxi driver

Cack   defecate
Cackelberry   egg
Cactus   broken, not working
Cadge   beg or borrow
Cagey   shy, wary
Cahoots   in partnership
Cake hole   mouth
Camp as a row of tents   a male homosexual
Camp oven   cast iron cooking pot
Can   a prison
Can of worms   problems, troublesome
Cancer stick   cigarette
Can-do   affirmative, yes
Cane toad   a person from Queensland
Caper   activity
Captain Cook   look
Carbie/Carby   carburetor
Cardie   cardigan
Cark it   to die
Carnie   carnival worker
Cash and carry   a supermarket
Cashed up   plenty of money
Chalkie   a school teacher
Champers   champagne
Chancy   uncertain, risky
Charge like a wounded bull   to charge excessively high prices
Cheese and kisses   wife
Cheesed off   very angry, annoyed
Cherry   a red cricket ball
Chew the fat   have a chat or conversation

Cooking in a **camp oven** is part of **Aussie outback** history and today the **camp oven** is used by campers.

Chewie   chewing gum

Chiack   taunt, tease

Chicken shit   no value, worthless

China plate   mate, pal, friend

Chin wag   have a chat, conversation

Chippie   a carpenter, wood worker

Chips   potato fries, crisps

Chock a block/Chockers   very full, overflowing

Chockie   chocolate

Chockie bikkies   chocolate biscuits

Choke a brown dog   something distasteful, bad food

Choof off   go now, get lost, leave

Chook   a chicken or fowl

Choppers   teeth, false teeth

Chrissie   Christmas time

Chrome dome   a bald man

Chuck   1. throw, toss; 2. vomit

Chuck a sickie   take a work sick day when you're not sick

Chuck it in   quit, give up, surrender

Chuffed   very happy

Chunder   to vomit

Clackers   false teeth

Clanger   1. a big lie; 2. a shock

Clapped out   worn out, old

Classer   a wool grader

Claytons   fake

Cleanskin   1. a bottle of wine without a label; 2. unbranded cattle

Clear as mud   confusing

Clever dick   1. a smart person; 2. a conceited person

Clicks, Klicks, K's   kilometres

Some **Aussies** still prefer to keep **chooks** in their backyards to provide **googies** rather than buy them from the grocery shop.

Clink   prison
Clobber   clothes
Clod hoppers   feet
Clucky, feeling   broody, maternal
Coat hanger   Sydney Harbour bridge
Cobber   work mate, friend, pal
Cock up   something gone wrong
Cockie   1. cockatoo; 2. farmer, grazier; 3. cockroach
Cocky's joy   golden syrup, treacle
Codger   a perculiar person, unusual
Cods   testicles
Coit   bum, anus
Coldie   a beer bottle or can

Cockies are cold-blooded pests who thrive in warm, humid conditions. They make their home wherever they find food, moisture and shelter.

Colonial goose   a boned leg of lamb seasoned with herbs and onion
Come a gutser   1. have an accident; 2. to make a mistake
Come in spinner   call for the tossing of the coins in the game of two-up
Come the raw prawn   pretend, be naive
Come to blows   start fighting
Common as dog shit   very common
Compo   workers compensation payment
Conk   nose
Conk out   engine breakdown
Conned   tricked, deceived
Cooee   a call; often used in the bush to locate lost persons
Cook   one's wife
Cooking with gas   doing very well
Cop   1. police officer; 2. obtain; 3. caught doing something wrong
Corker   something astonishing or striking
Corroboree   a ceremonial meeting of Australian Aborigines
Cossie   swimming costume

Couldn't lie straight in bed   a cheat, liar

Counter lunch/countery   pub lunch

Country cousin   a dozen, twelve

Cove   a man, bloke or chap

Cow cocky   dairy farmer

Cow of a thing   frustrating or upsetting

Crack a fat   get an erection

Crack of dawn   first light of day

Crack onto   make a pass or pursue someone romantically

Cracker   the tip of a stock whip

Cranky   angry, in a bad mood

Creamed   soundly beaten in sport

Creek   a small stream

Crikey   an expression of astonishment

Crim   a criminal

Australia has two different species of **crocs**, both of which are native to tropical Queensland.

Croak   to die

Croc   crocodile

Crook   1. unwell; 2. no good, bad, rotten

Crook as Rookwood   sick (Rookwood being a cemetery)

Cropper, came a   fall over

Crow bar   a large lever

Crow eater   a South Australian

Crown jewels   testicles

Crud   dirt, rubbish

Cruet   the head

Cubby house   a small house made for children to play in

Cunning as a shit house rat   a very cunning person

Cuppa   a cup of tea or coffee

Curly   nickname for a bald person

Cut lunch   sandwiches or pre-packed lunch

Cut snake, mad as a   1. very upset; 2. crazy
Cut the crap   stop talking rubbish
Cut up   1. upset, distressed; 2. criticise
Dab hand at   good at, skilled
Dacks/Daks   1.trousers, pants; 2. underpants
Dad and Dave   a shave
Daddy long legs   a long-legged spider
Dag   1. an amusing person; 2. dry excreta hanging from a sheep's wool
Daggy   1. untidy; 2. dirty; 3. uncool, lacking style
Dago   war-time name for Italians
Daily grind   monotonous work
Dakka   marijuana, pot, dope
Damper   bread made from flour and water usually cooked in a camp oven
Dangle   to die by hanging, to hang
Dangle the carrot   offer a bribe, tempt
Darl   darling
Dart   a cigarette
Darwin shuffle   tax avoidance scheme
Darwin stubbie   a very large beer bottle
Date   anus
Date roller   roll of toilet paper
Dazzler   brilliant, good
Dead as mutton   very dead
Dead beat   very tired
Dead heart   the arid centre of Australia
Dead horse   tomato sauce
Dead marine   empty beer bottle
Dead on   correct
Dead ringer   a close resemblance of someone else
Dead set   correct, spot on, a sure thing

Uluru is situated in the **dead heart** of Australia.

Deadbeat   1. loser, lazy person; 2. one who doesn't pay their debts
Deadly   fantastic, great, awesome
Dee   a detective
Demo   a demonstration
Dero/Derro   a derelict, vagrant dependant on alcohol
Dial   your face
Dibs   marbles
Dice   throw away, reject
Dicey   unreliable
Dickhead   jerk, annoying person, idiot
Dickory dock   clock
Diddle   to cheat, swindle
Diddler   swindler
Dig me   I've done well, excelled
Dig you   you've done well, excelled
Digger   an Australian soldier
Dill   a stupid person
Dilly bag   a small bag to carry sugar, tea, etc
Ding   a minor motor accident
Ding bat   a fool, silly person
Ding dong   a major fight
Dinger   anus, backside
Dingo   an Australian native dog
Dink   to carry a second person on a bike, motorcycle or horse
Dinky-di   the genuine article
Dinkum   no joke, the real thing
Dip out   1. miss out; 2. to refuse a drink
Dipstick   idiot, a loser
Divvy up   share out equally
Dob in   1. tell on someone, report; 2. contribute to a fund

The **Dingo** is **Oz's** wild dog. It is medium in size with a red to yellow coat and bushy tail. **Dingos** don't bark but they howl.

Docket   receipt, bill

Doco   a documentary

Dodgy   something suspicious

Dog and bone   phone

Dog box   a compartment in a train carriage

Dog fence   to keep dingoes out of pastoral country

Dogger   a dingo hunter

Dog's balls, stands out like   very obvious

Dog's breakfast   a real mess, confusion, turmoil

Dog's eye   a meat pie

Dole   social security payment

A **dog's eye** is a small meat pie often containing minced or diced meat and gravy. Sometimes smothered with **dead horse**, it is an iconic **Aussie take-away** food snack.

Dole bludger   won't work and being supported by the government

Dolled up   women dressed smartly

Done like a dinner   beaten in sport or a fight

Donga/Donger   a penis

Donk   a boat or car engine

Doodle   a penis

Doona   duvet

Doovalacky   used when you can't remember what something is called

Doover   1. a penis; 2. a thing

Dork   1. a penis; 2. someone who is uncool

Dose, a   venereal disease

Down a few   have a few drinks

Down the hatch   drink up

Down under   Australia

Drag Queen   transvestite, dresses as a woman

Drag the chain   to be slow, lag behind

Dray   a wagon, horse cart

Driza-bone   a weatherproof coat or jacket

Drongo   a stupid person

Drop a fart   to pass wind

Drop kick   a useless person

Drop your guts   to fart

Drover   stock moving contractor, stockman

Drum   1. give information or advice; 2. to organise

Dry as a dead dingo's donger   very dry, thirsty

Dry rots   diarrhoea, the trots

Duchess   dressing table, sideboard

Duck's guts   a very good thing

Duckshove   pass responsibilities off to others

Dudds   male clothing

Duff   1. mess up; 2. steal cattle

Duff, up the   pregnant

Duffer   stupid person, unthinking

Duffing   stealing cattle or sheep

Dummy, spit the   have a tantrum

Dump   1. poorly kept house; 2. act of defecation; 3. end a relationship

Dumper   a large wave breaking onto a beach

Dunny   a toilet; indoor or outdoor

Dunny diver   a plumber

Dunny paper   toilet paper

Durry   a cigarette

Dust up   brawl or fight

Dutch oven   farting under the bed sheets

Dux   top of the class

Toilet paper is referred to as **dunny paper** however, in the early days, most **dunny paper** was actually torn up sheets of newspaper.

Eager beaver   a keen person

Eagle eyes   very good eyesight

Eagle hawking   plucking wool from dead sheep

Eagle shits   getting paid

Ear bashing   persistent talking, nagging

Earful   1. oral advice; 2. stern reprimand

Early bird   1. get up early; 2. arrive early

Early mark   leave work before normal finishing time

Earn a quid   working for a living, making money

Ears flapping   eavesdropping, listening in

Easy   1. to have no firm preference; 2. promiscuous

Easy lay   a woman with loose morals

Easy-peasy   very easy

Eat a horse   very hungry

Eat a horse and chase the rider   indicating one's great hunger

Eat crow   embarrassment when a plan has failed or backfired

Edgy   nervous

Egg beater   helicopter

Egg head   an intellectual person

Ekka   the Brisbane Agricultural Exhibition

Elbow grease   hard work

El-cheapo   1. something very cheap; 2. inferior quality

Elevator   lift

Emcee   master of ceremony

Empties   empty beer bottles

Emu   a racecourse person who picks up discarded betting tickets

Emu-bobber   someone employed to pick up rubbish after a function

Emu parade   group of people employed to clean up after large gatherings

Entree   appetiser, starter

Enzed/NZ   an acronym, New Zealand

Enzedder   a New Zealander

Esky   a portable insulated container used to keep food and drink cool

Even stevens   1. equal; 2. not owed anything

Even the score   revenge

Every dog has its day   opportunities come your way

E

Every man and his dog   a general public crowd

Every Tom, Dick and Harry   a general public crowd

Every which way   all directions

Ex   one's former wife, husband, girlfriend or boyfriend

Exchange notes   to gossip

Excuse the French   apology for bad language

Expecting   pregnant

Exy   expensive

Eye off   to look at with interest

Every Tom, Dick and Harry was at the opening of the new shopping centre.

Eyeball to eyeball   face to face

Eyes like road maps   bloodshot after a big night out

Eyesore   offensive, ugly

FJ   a popular model of the Holden car 1953-1956

Fab   fabulous, wonderful, great

Face ache   irritating person

Face fungus   a beard

Face like a festered pimple   1. acute acne; 2. ugly

Face, off one's   drunk

Fag   1. a cigarette; 2. a homosexual

Fagged out   tired

Fair and square   honest, trustworthy

Fair crack of the whip   to be treated fairly, asking for a fair chance

Fair dinkum   real, true

Fair enough   agreeing about something

Fair go mate   give a chance

Fair suck of the sav   1. a fair go; 2. exclamation of wonder or disbelief

Fairy   homosexual male

Fairy floss   cotton candy, candy floss

Falsies   1. fake breasts; 2. false teeth

Famished   very hungry

Fangs   teeth
Fanny   a vagina
Far flung   remote, far away
Fart sack   1. a bed or bunk; 2. a sleeping bag
Fart-arse   waste time
Farts like a two-stroke   loud flatulence
Fat cake   damper fried in fat
Favourite poison   preferred alcoholic drink
Feel crook   unwell
Feel horny   sexually aroused
Fell off the back of a truck   stolen property
Fella   a male person
Feral   a hippie
Fergie/Fergy   a Ferguson tractor
Ferret   a penis
Few and far between   rare, not common
Fib   a lie, untruth
Fibber   a liar
Fiddle   to cheat
Fiddler   a swindler
Fifty-fifty   equal amounts
Figjam   *uck I'm good just ask me; high opinion of oneself
Filly   1. a young girl; 2. female horse
Filthy rich   very wealthy
Finicky   fastidious
Fins   the arms
Fire away   begin to speak
Fire blanks   a sterile male
Firebug   arsonist
First cab off the rank   first in line

Feral Meryl believes the way to peace is through love and tolerance.

First fleeter   a person who can be traced back to the first fleet
First thing   early morning
Fish out of water   uncomfortable with other people or surroundings
Fisho   a fishmonger
Fit as a mallee bull   a very fit person
Fits like a glove   suitable, a good fit
Five o'clock shadow   beard growth on a man's face
Five finger discount   shop lifting
Fizzer   1. a failure; 2. fiasco
Flak   criticism
Flake   shark's flesh; commonly sold in fish and chip shops
Flake out   lie down, to sleep
Flame   girlfriend, sweetheart
Flamin'   1. very good; 2. very bad
Flap your gums   talk too much
Flash a brown eye   expose ones bare backside, anus
Flasher   a man who exposes his genitals in public

Fred the **flasher.**

Flat as a tack   1. tired, worn out; 2. anything that is flat
Flat broke   having no money
Flat chat   as fast as possible
Flat out like a lizard drinking   a very busy person, working hard
Flatfoot   a policeman
Flatties   low-heeled shoes
Flea bag   infested with fleas
Flea-house   cinema, picture theatre
Flesh and blood   family, kin, offspring
Flick   1. getting rid of something; 2. movie
Flick it on   sell something soon after buying for a quick profit
Flippers   hands
Floater   1. a meat pie in a plate of gravy; 2. faeces floating in a toilet

Flog   1. to sell something; 2. to steal something

Flogging a dead horse   trying to do something when it won't work

Floozie   a promiscuous woman

Fluke   to win by chance

Flunk   to fail

Flutter   place a small bet

Fly the coop   1. escape; 2. leave home

Flyblown   maggots on meat

Flying fox   a cable car

Fob off   1. dismiss; 2. be rude to someone

Foggiest   no idea or clue

Snowy took **forty winks** during **smoko** because he couldn't keep his **peepers** open.

Fool's gold   pyrites; a mineral that resembles gold

Foot the bill   pay the costs

Footpath   sidewalk

Footslogger   a soldier

Footy   term for Australian rules football, rugby league or rugby union

For keeps   permanently own

Fork over   pay a bet, hand over something

Forty winks   a short nap or sleep

Fossick   search for gold or gemstones

Fossil   an old person

Foulmouthed   using obscene language

Four eyes   a person who wears glasses

Four letter word   any vulgar words having four letters

Four-b-two/four   a piece of timber

Foursome   four people in a party

Franger   a condom

Freckle   the anus

Fred Nerk   an imaginary person

Free loader   a person who uses somebody's hospitality, food and drink

Freebie   something for nothing

Free-for-all   a fight involving many people

Freeze the balls off a brass monkey   very cold, frosty

Fremantle Doctor   Perth breeze from the direction of Fremantle

Frenchie   a condom

Freo   Fremantle, Western Australia

Freshie   a fresh water crocodile

Fridge   a refrigerator

Fried eggs   flat breasts

Frig   to masturbate

Frigging   masturbating

Frigid   an unresponsive person

Frillie   a frill-necked lizard

Fringe benefit   extra rewards above regular wage

Frisky   sexually aroused

Frog   a French person

Frog and toad   road

Frogshit   insincere talk, nonsense

From a to z   from the beginning to the end

From arsehole to breakfast time   1. all over; 2. completely covered

From go to whoa   from the beginning to the end

From pillar to post   roaming from one place to another

From scratch   from nothing

Fruit for the sideboard   perks, rewards, bonus

Fruitloop   a crazy person

Fuddy-duddy   1. conservative; 2. a fussy person

Full as a boot   very drunk, intoxicated

Full bore   to go all out

Full frontal   a naked body from front on

Full of beans   very energetic

The **fridge** was absolutely **chockers** with drinks and **tucker**.

Full of shit   talking rubbish
Full on   most intense
Full quid   sane
Fungus face   a male with a beard
Furphy   1. originally a water cart; 2. a rumour or a false report, a lie
Fuss pot   1. a person who worries a lot; 2. a very fussy person
Fuzz   the police
Fuzzy-headed   a bad hangover
Fuzzy wuzzy angel   WWII stretcher bearer from Papua New Guinea
G'day/Gidday   Good-day, hello
Ga Ga   mad, silly
Gab   chatter, talk
Gabba   Queensland Cricket Ground at Wooloongabba, Brisbane
Gadabout   a person having an active social life
Gag   a joke
Galah   1. native Australian parrot; 2. a fool, idiot
Gallops   thoroughbred horse races
Galoot   a stupid clumsy person
Galvo   galvanized iron
Game as a piss ant   a very daring person
Game as Ned Kelly   very daring
Games up   the end of an activity
Gammy   crippled, lame
Gander   have a look at something
Gangie   group sex
Ganja   marijuana
Gaol bird   habitual criminal
Garbage guts   a greedy person
Garbo   garbage or waste collector
Gas bagging   talk at great length non-stop.

Ned Kelly is an **Aussie** folk hero yet he was a criminal. He is remembered today in the popular expression, "as **game as Ned Kelly**".

Gasper   a cigarette
Gawk   stare openly
Gear   clothes, uniform
Gee gee   a horse
Geek   have a look
Genny   a generator
Gents   a public toilet for men only
German band   your hand
Get a bit   have sexual intercourse
Get a dose   contract a venereal disease
Get a leg in the door   make headway
Get a wriggle on   hurry up
Get nicked   exclamation of contempt
Get off at Redfern   withdraw before ejaculation
Get rooted   a term of abuse; go away!
Get stuffed   a term of abuse; go away, piss off!
Get stuck into   1. abuse someone; 2. eat hungrily; 3. do a task with vigour
Get the arse   to be fired/sacked
Get the big A   to be fired/sacked
Get the nod   get approval, the go ahead
Get the rough end of the pineapple   worst treatment
Get the shits   get upset
Gibber   a round stone, a small rock
Gig   1. performance at a venue; 2. gigabyte
Gimme   give me
Give the game away   to abandon interest
Give it a burl   to try, have a go
Give it a miss   change one's mind
Give lip   cheeky, answer back
Glad rags   your best clothes

Jo and Flo spent most of the day **gas bagging** about the new **bloke** at the office.

Glass of amber   a glass of beer

Go ape shit   become very angry

Go bad   1. down on one's luck; 2. a bad joke that is not appreciated

Go down like a lead balloon   failure

Go Dutch   pay your own way

Go for a burn   1. to drive fast; 2. test drive

Go for a snake hiss   a male to urinate

Go like the clappers   move fast

Go off half-cocked   not thinking straight

Go to buggery   ask someone to leave in a very nasty way

Go walkabout   wandering off

Goanna   a piano

Gob   mouth

Gobful, give a   to abuse

Gobsmacked   astounded, flabbergasted

Goer   1. an energetic person; 2. go ahead with something

Going off   used to describe a fun night spot or party

Gone to billyo   disappeared

Gone to the dogs   going from good to bad

Good as gold   something very good

Good monger   good food

Good oil   correct information

Good on ya   well done

Good sort   a good looking woman

Goog, as full as a   1. drunk; 2. full of food

Googie   an egg

Goolies   testicles

Goss   gossip

Grab forty winks   have a nap

Grazier   pastoral property owner

Nothing beats a boiled **googie** for **brekkie**.

Greasy   a bad cook

Great Australian salute   the action of shooing flies away with your hand

Green around the gills   feeling sick

Green thumb   able to make any plant grow

Greenie   an environmentalist

Grizzle   to complain

Grog   alcohol

Grommet   a teenage surfer

Grot   an untidy person

Grouse   very good, terrific

Grub   1. food; 2. a meal; 3. a dirty eater; 4. a dirty child

Grundies   underwear (from television and media mogul, Reg Grundy)

Grunt   power, strength

Gully   a very small valley

Gummies   gumboots

Gun   1. best at something; 2. accelerate a vehicle

Gunna   all talk and no action

Gunyah   an aboriginal shelter

Gutful   had enough

Gutful of piss   drunk

Gutsy   brave, fearsome

Guttersnipe   a gossiper

Gutzer   to fall over, trip

Guzzler   a heavy drinker

Gyno   a gynecologist

Barry **hoed into** a big plate of **grub** for **tea**.

Hack   1. a taxi; 2. horse

Had a few too many   too many alcoholic drinks

Had a good innings   a good life

Had a skin full   drinks too much

Had it   1. run out of patience; 2. dead

Had it soft   an easy time
Hair of the dog   a drink to cure a hangover
Half shot   nearly intoxicated
Half time   the middle of a team sport's game
Half your luck   very lucky
Half-mast   trousers that don't reach the ankles
Ham and eggs   legs
Hammer and tongs   worked very hard
Hammy   hamstring
Hand   a hired worker
Hand in hand   worked together
Hand in the till   stealing from employer
Hand the hat around   giving to a cause
Hand-me-downs   passed on clothing
Handy   skilled, clever
Hang around like a bad smell   not wanted around
Hang on a tick   wait a minute
Hanger-on   a free loader
Hankie   handkerchief
Happy as a pig in shit   very happy
Happy as Larry   extremely happy
Happy little vegemite   someone in a good mood
Hard word on   1. to ask a favour; 2. to ask a sexual favour
Hassle   1. a problem; 2. inconvenience
Hate someone's guts   dislike someone
Haul   ill gotten goods
Haunt   favourite place
Have a ball   a very good time
Have a bang   have sexual intercourse
Have a barney   a fight

Have a bo-peep   have a look
Have a burl   attempt something
Have a crack   attempt
Have a decko/dekko   have a look
Have a domestic   a family argument
Have a flutter   a small bet, wager
Have a gander   have a look
Have a go   try something
Have a heart   have mercy
Have a pash   long, passionate kiss
Have a prang   car smash, accident
Have a shot at   to try something
Have a snort   have an alcoholic drink
Have a spell   a rest from work
Have a splash   have a bet, wager
Have a stab at   attempt something
Have a tub   bath or wash

Bluey decided to **have a tub** to soothe his aching body after a day of hard **yakka**.

Have long arms and short pockets   to be a miser, stingy
Haven't got a brass razoo   broke, no money
Hayburner   a horse
Head in the sand   to ignore reality
Heads and tails   used in the game of two-up
Heaps   a lot, a large amount
Heard it all before   same thing over and over
Heart of gold   1. generous; 2. helpful
Heart of stone   mean, unemotional
Heart starter   early morning alcoholic drink, strong coffee, first cigarette
Heart stopper   shocking, terrifying
Heavies   minders, bodyguards
Heebie-jeebies   tension, nervousness

Heifers   young female cattle
Hell for leather   fast, speeding
Hemp   marijuana
Hen-pecked   dominated by a wife
Hen's night   bachelorette party
Hen's teeth   scarce
Here to stay   permanent
Herk   vomit
Hey   greeting
Hick   country person
Hickey   a love bite
Hidey hole   a secret hiding place
High and dry   abandoned, alone
High as a kite   1. under the influence of drugs or alcohol; 2. in high spirits
High flying   doing well in business
High on the nose   stinking, smelly
Highfaluting   snobbish, pompous, pretentious
His nibs   the boss, one in charge
Hit and giggle   tennis
Hit and miss   careless
Hit the frog and toad   depart
Hit the hay   go to bed
Hit the headlines   achieve fame
Hit the jackpot   very lucky
Hit the nail on the head   exactly right
Hit the piss   drink heavily
Hit the roof   become angry
Hit the sack   go to bed
Hit the slops   get on the booze
Hit the toe   depart, go

Jack **hit the slops** every night at his local **watering hole** before heading home to **cop** an **ear bashing** from the **ball and chain**.

Hiya   greeting
Hobbles   straps used to tie horses' legs
Hoe into   start eating
Hold the reins   be in charge
Hollies/Hols   holidays
Holy dooley   exclamation indicating surprise, indignation
Holy mackerel   exclamation indicating surprise, indignation
Holy smoke   exclamation indicating surprise, indignation
Home and hosed   easy winner; foregone conclusion, successful finish
Homely   1. plain; 2. cosy, snug
Homestead   the main house on a property
Homo   a homosexual man
Honk   1. the nose; 2. blow a car's horn
Honkers   Hong Kong
Hooch   marijuana
Hoof it   to walk, run
Hooks   fingers
Hooley   a wild party
Hoon   a reckless show off
Hoop   a jockey
Hooray   1. goodbye; 2. pleasure
Hooroo   goodbye
Hop it   go away
Hopping mad   very angry
Hops   beer
Horn   1. an erection; 2. a telephone
Horn in   enter a discussion uninvited
Horse and cart   a fart
Horse around   play up
Horse sense   common sense

Bazza was **hopping mad** when he noticed that some **galoot** had **pranged** into the side of his new car.

Horse play   rough behaviour
Horses for courses   suited to the task
Horse's hoof   homosexual
Hostie   air hostess, flight attendant
Hot air   pretentious, empty talk
Hot to trot   eager to start
Hot foot it   go, depart, leave
Hot pants   a woman with strong sexual desires
Hot under the collar   very angry
Hotel   a pub
Hottie   1. a hot water bottle; 2. a sexy person
House of ill fame   a brothel
How about it?   asking for sex
How come?   why
How ya goin?   greeting
How's it going?   greeting
How's things?   greeting
Howzat?   an appeal for approval
Hoy   attract attention

According to **every Tom, Dick and Harry**, Brenda was a **bloody bonzer hostie** and a real **hottie.**

Hubby   husband
Huey   another name for God, the powers above
Humbug   1. a striped lolly; 2. a cheat
Humdinger   very good, the best
Hump   1. carry something; 2. lift; 3. have sex
Humpy   a rough bush shelter
Hung over   feeling poorly after a drinking binge
Hurl   vomit
Husband beater   a rolling pin
Hush money   a bribe
Hush up   keep quiet

Hustle   to obtain money illegally

Hype   overdone

Hyped up/Hypo   over excited

I.O.U   "I owe you", a written confirmation of debt

I kid you not   declaration that one is speaking the truth

I'll be   exclamation of surprise

I'll drink to that   agree, approve

I'm all right Jack   ok

I've had it   complete frustration

Ice block/Icy pole   popsicle

Icing on the cake   best finish

Icky   1. offensive; 2. risky

Idiot box   a television set

Idle rich   very wealthy people

Iffy   suspicious

Illywhacker   a small time trickster, crook

Imp   a naughty child

In a jiff/jiffy   soon, a short time

In a spin   confused

In a spot of bother   in trouble

In a tic   soon

In cloudland   not concentrating

In cog   in disguise, incognito

In droves   big numbers

In fine feathers   full of vitality

In fits and starts   irregular

In for the kill   defeat

In good nick   good condition

In hock   in debt

In house   associated to members of a house or club

An **ice block** is a sweet cold confection consisting of ice cream or flavoured water frozen on a stick.

In like Flynn   1. a sure thing; 2. sexual success (referring to Errol Flynn)
In strife   in trouble
In the bag   success
In the box seat   successful position
In the can   in prison
In the chair   next to buy a round of drinks
In the clink   in gaol
In the cooler   in gaol
In the cot   in bed
In the doghouse   out of favour with your wife, husband or partner
In the drink   in water
In the family way   pregnant
In the good books   in favour
In the grip of the grape   addicted to wine
In the guts   in the centre, middle
In the know   inside information
In the nuddy   naked
In the raw   naked, nude
In the red   in debt
In the right place at the right time   in a good position
In the same boat   in the same situation, face the same challenges
In the shit   in serious trouble
In the sticks   remote areas in the bush
In the wars   1. minor injuries; 2. arguments
In tow   following someone
In trouble   pregnant
Indian giver   give a gift to someone then take it back
Info   information
In-laws   relatives by marriage
Inside job   a crime within an organisation

Into thin air   disappear
Intro   introduction
Irish curtains   cobwebs
Iron clad   safe
Iron fisted   ruthless, severe
Iron oneself out   get drunk
Iron underpants   girdles, step-ins
Irrits   the shits
Is it a goer?   will it happen?
Is the Pope Catholic?   yes
It   could be male or female
It's a goer   1. will happen; 2. proceed
It's in the cards   may happen
It's sweet   all is ok
It's your funeral   your fault
It never rains but it pours   lots of things happen at once
Itchy feet   need to travel
Itsy-bitsy   very small, tiny
Ivories   teeth, false teeth
J.P.   a Justice of the Peace
Jab   an injection
Jabber   to talk rapidly
Jack dancer   cancer
Jack in the box   someone who cannot sit still
Jack of all trades   someone who can do all jobs
Jacked off   1. annoyed; 2. disgusted; 3. frustrated
Jack Shay   to stay
Jack shit   nothing
Jack up   1. refuse to work; 2. disobey
Jackass   1. kookaburra; 2. an idiot

Yes, the Pope is Catholic.

Jacked off   1. annoyed; 2. masturbated
Jackeroo   a male stock hand
Jackie/Jacky   kookaburra
Jacky Howe   a sleeveless garment worn by labourers
Jaffle   a toasted sandwich
Jake   okay, alright
Jam tart   sweetheart
Jammed in   over-crowded
Jargon   nonsense, meaningless talk
Jarmies   pyjamas, night dress
Jay-cee   Jesus Christ
Jelly   1. gelatin desert, jello; 2. gelignite, explosive
Jerk   a fool
Jerkin the gherkin   to masturbate
Jerry built   badly built
Jiffy   very short time
Jiggered   broken, spoiled
Jillaroo   a female stock hand
Jimmy Woodser   a person who drinks on their own in a bar
Jingoes   exclamation of surprise
Jittery   nervous, anxious
Job somebody   to hit someone, fight
Jock   genital support worn by sportsmen
Jockeys   male underpants
Jocks   male underpants
Joe Blake   a snake
Joe Bloggs   anybody
Joe Blow   an ordinary bloke
Joey   baby kangaroo
John   1. a policeman; 2. a toilet; 3. prostitute's client

Johnny cake 1. damper; 2. bush cakes
Johnny come lately a recent arrival
Join up enlist for military service
Joint a house, place, abode
Joker 1. a person who is amusing; 2. a person you're unsure about
Jollies sexual excitement
Jonah to bring bad luck
Journo a journalist
Joy ride an enjoyable ride
Jug 1. prison; 2. measure of beer served in a large glass jug
Juggle the pennies budget
Jugs breasts, boobs
Juice petrol, gas
Jumble sale a sale of second-hand items
Jumbuck a sheep
Jump at it 1. chance it; 2. offered a job
Jump bail abscond after paying bail
Jump in and out of bed be very promiscuous
Jump in the lake go away, piss off
Jump start get a good start
Jump the gun start too soon
Jump the queue jump in front of someone in line
Jump the rattler ride the train illegally
Jumper 1. sweater, pullover; 2. commit suicide by jumping from a height
Jump up and down 1. make a fuss; 2. strongly protest
Jumpy nervous, tense
Jungle juice home-made inferior alcoholic drink
Junk anything that is worthless
Junk food take-away food
Jump the gun gain an unfair advantage by starting prematurely

Jumbuck is an **Aussie** term for sheep and is featured in the famous poem and song, "Waltzing Matilda".

Just down the street   not far away
Just my luck   frustration
Just what the doctor ordered   exactly what is required
K's   kilometres
Kafuffle   a commotion
Kamikaze   a reckless act
Kanaka   a Pacific Islander (seldom used)
Kanakas   testicles
Kanga   1. kangaroo; 2. shoe
Kaput   1. broken, smashed; 2. is dead
Kark   1. die; 2. broken, ruined
Keel over   1. to fall over; 2. die; 3. faint
Keen as mustard   very enthusiastic
Keen on someone   attracted to someone
Keep a low profile   keep away from publicity
Keep an eye on everything   watch over, look after
Keep back   restrain, withhold
Keep in touch   maintain a friendship
Keep it in the family   keep secrets within a family
Keep on the ball   constant alertness
Keep one's chin up   maintain good spirits, courage
Keep one's head above water   survive at all costs
Keep one's mouth shut   refrain from speaking out
Keep your shirt on   settle down, take it easy
Keg   a barrel of beer
Kelpie   an Australian sheepdog
Kero   kerosene
Khyber pass   arse, bum
Kick   1. pleasurable thrill; 2. strong alcohol taste; 3. trouser pocket
Kick arse   totally amazing

Kick back   relax
Kick in   1. to contribute; 2. buy a drink
Kick in the arse   a severe scolding
Kick in the teeth   a severe setback
Kick off   commence to play sport; football, soccer
Kick on   to continue
Kick the bucket   to die
Kick the tin   1. donate; 2. buy a round of drinks
Kick up one's heels   have fun
Kiddo   to address a young person
Kicking up a shinty   making an angry fuss
Kill a brown dog   potent, deadly
Kill a snake   urinate
Kill the goose that lays the golden eggs   end something profitable
Killer, a   a sheep or cow killed for meat on a property
Kimberley cool   the coolness beer reaches when immersed in a water bag
Kimberley formal   men's dress style; shirt, shorts, socks and shoes
Kimberley mutton   wild goat roasted
Kindie   kindergarten
King Dick   1. the best; 2. above ordinary people
King hit   a surprise punch in the head
King pin   a boss or leader
Kink   1. a cramp, twinge; 2. a sexual pervert
Kinky   unusual sexual tastes
Kip   1. a small thin piece of flat wood used to toss coins in a game of two-up
Kip   2. a short sleep
Kiwi   a New Zealander
Klicks   kilometres
Knackered   very tired
Knackers   testicles

Knee high to a grasshopper   a short person
Knee trembler   1. frightening; 2. sexual intercourse standing up
Knickers   underpants for women
Knick knacks   trinkets, bric a brac
Knife in the back   a betrayal
Knob   1. penis; 2. annoying or stupid person, dickhead
Knock   to criticise
Knock back   1. a refusal, a rebuff; 2. consume a drink
Knock down   1. reduce the price; 2. spend freely on liquor
Knock it off   1. stop it!; 2. euphemism for sexual intercourse
Knock off   1. stop work; 2. steal something; 3. make a copy
Knock shop   a brothel
Knock up   1. make pregnant; 2. construct; 3. cook hastily; 4. exhaust
Knocked up   pregnant
Knocker   one who derides all ideas, things and projects
Knuckle down   show willing to work
Knuckle sandwich   a bunch of fives, a punch to the teeth
Knuckle, to go the   to fight, to punch
Kombi   a small van, wagon
Konk   nose
Koori   an aborigine
Kosher   the real thing
Kybosh   rubbish, nonsense
Lab   laboratory
Lace into   attack, abuse
Ladies   womens' toilet

Dave discovered that Gary had been **eyeing off** his **flame** and threatened him with a **knuckle sandwich**.

Ladies man   a man attracted to women
Lady muck   a snobby woman
Lady's waist   either a 5 or 7 ounce glass of beer
Lag   a habitual criminal, convict

Lagerphone   a musical instrument made of bottle tops nailed to a stick

Lagger   a police informer

Laid up   sick, bedridden

Laid back   relaxed

Lair/Lairy   1. a flashy male; 2. vulgar person; 3. show off

Lamington   small square sponge cake coated in chocolate icing and coconut

Lappy   a laptop

Larrikin   a prankster, hooligan

Lash at, have a   to make an attempt at something

Lash out   1. spend freely; 2. burst into violent action or criticise severely

Last resort   a final option

Laugh at the lawn   to vomit

Laughing gear   the mouth

Laughing jackass   a kookaburra

Lav/Lavvy   outdoor toilet, any toilet

Lay   a person considered as a sex object, a good lay

Lay a cable   to defecate

Lay down the law   what I say goes, the boss

Lay in the hay   have sexual intercourse

Lay into   to beat up, abuse

Lay low   stay out of site

Lay off   1. ease up, stop; 2. be sacked

Layabout   a lazy person

Lay-down misere   it's a certainty

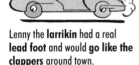

Lenny the **larrikin** had a real **lead foot** and would **go like the clappers** around town.

Lazy Susan   a revolving centre tray on a dining table

Lead a dog's life   an unhappy life

Lead feet/foot   to drive too fast, a reckless driver

Leak   to urinate

Learner   a person learning to drive a motor vehicle

Leave it at that   end of story, say no more in conversation

Left to the wolves   deserted
Left footer   a Catholic
Leg it   to walk or run
Legal eagle   a lawyer or solicitor
Legless   very drunk
Lemon   1. shoddy work; 2. a faulty car
Lend of, to have a   take advantage of a gullible person
Lezzo/Lesbo   a Lesbian
Let 'er rip   an enthusiastic start of something
Let one's hair down   behave in an informal manner
Let sleeping dogs lie   cause no further trouble
Let slip   to reveal a secret
Lick into shape   repair, fix up
Lick the dust   to die or be wounded
Licked   to be beaten or defeated
Lid   a hat
Lie doggo   1. to hide away; 2. get out of something
Lie in   stay in bed, get up late
Lie low   stay out of site
Life of Riley   a trouble free existence
Light on   horse racing short weight
Like a shag on a rock   1. a loner; 2. out of place
Like buggery   no way
Like the clappers   very fast
Line 'em up   lining up a round of drinks
Lingo   language
Lippy   lipstick
Lizard drinking, flat out like a   very busy
Loaded   1. very wealthy; 2. under the effects of alcohol or drugs, stoned
Lob/Lob in   1. arrive unannounced; 2. drop in to see someone

Lollies   candy, sweets

Longneck   750ml bottle of beer in South Australia

Lucky country, the   Australia

Lug   1. carry; 2. ear; 3. clumsy person

Lurk   1. underhanded racket; 2. scheme; 3. on to a good thing

Mad as a cut snake   crazy, insane

Mad as a meat axe   extremely mad

Mag   magazine

Maggie   magpie

Maidenhood   virginity

Make a blue   make a mistake, error

Make a quid   earn a living, wage, salary

Make it snappy   hurry up

Make tracks   depart, leave

Make waves   to cause trouble

Makings, the   tobacco and cigarette papers, to roll your own

Malarky   foolish talk, raving on, idle gossip

Mallee   unpopulated scrub or bushland

Mallee bull, fit as a   very strong, fit

Man in white   a cricket umpire

Man on the land   a farmer or grazier

Manchester   household linen

Man's best friend   1. his dog; 2. his penis

Manual   a car with a manual gear shift

March down the aisle   to get married

Marching orders   getting the sack, to be fired

Marge   margarine

Marriage on the rocks   a marriage break up

Marties   tomatoes

Mary's room   the toilet

"The Lucky Country" is a nickname used to describe Australia, taken from the 1964 book by the same name by social critic Donald Horne.

Mash   mashed potatoes
Mate   close friend
Mate's rate   cheaper than usual price for a friend
Matilda   a blanket roll, a swag
Metho   methylated spirits
Middy   a 10 ounce glass of beer (NSW and Western Australia)
Mike   a microphone
Milk bar   corner store that usually sells take-away food
Milko   milkman
Mince pies   the eyes
Min-min light   a strange light that appears in outback Queensland
Missus, the   a man's spouse, wife
Mite   a small child, infant
Mitt   a hand or fist
Mo   moustache
Mob   1. cattle or sheep herd; 2. group of people
Mog/Moggy   a cat
Molly dooker   a left-handed person
Money bags   a rich person
Mongrel   1. mixed-breed dog; 2. despicable person; 3. something difficult
Moniker   a person's name
Monkey suit   a dinner suit
Moo   a silly woman
Moo juice   milk
Moolah   cash, money
Moosh   mouth
Mozzie   a mosquito
Muddie   a Queensland mud crab
Mudmap   a map or a sketch drawn on the ground
Muff   female genitals

Mug   1. face; 2. one who is easily fooled; 3. friendly insult
Mulga   the outback bush
Mullock   spoil or rock tailings from a mine
Munga   food
Murphy   a potato
Mushie   a mushroom
Muso   a musician
Muster   to herd or gather cattle or sheep
Mutt   a mongrel dog
Mutton head   a foolish person
My oath   total agreement
Mystery bags   sausages or snags

Bevan was a **muso** with **bloody** big dreams but spent most of his life **flat broke.**

Myxo   myxomatosis, viral disease introduced to deplete rabbit population
NBG   no bloody good
NRL   National rugby league
Nab   arrest, capture
Nada   **1.** nothing, zero, zip; 2. free
Nag   1. old inferior horse; 2. talk incessantly
Nail   1. catch, seize; 2. kill; 3. do something perfectly
Nail-biter   an exciting match or game with a close finish
Nana/Narna   a banana
Nanna/Nanny/Nannie   grandmother
Nappy   diaper
Nark   a person who nags and irritates continually
Narky   short-tempered
Nasho   national serviceman
Natter   chat, gossip
Naughty, have a   have sex
Near-at-hand   close by
Neato   excellent, great

Neddies   racing horses
Never never   desert regions of Australia
New chum   1. a newcomer; 2. beginner
Newbie   a newcomer to anything
Newsagent   a shop where you buy newspapers, magazines and books
Nibbles   a snack, small tit-bits of food
Nice drop   a good wine
Nick   to steal
Nick off   depart, go away
Nickers   women's underpants
Nigel   unpopular person, has no friends
Niggly   annoyed, angry
Night on the town   a big night out
Nineteenth hole   a bar in the golf club house
Nipper   1. a small crab or prawn; 2. a young child; 3. a young surf lifesaver
Nippy   1. cold; 2. active person
Nitwit   foolish person
No drama   no problem
No hoper   a fool, a person without merit
No room to swing a cat   a small room, cramped quarters
No worries   no problem
Nob   1. annoying person; 2. head; 3. elite person
Nod off   to fall asleep, have a nap
Noggin   the head
Nong   an idiot
Nope   no
Norks   breasts
North and South   mouth
Nosebag   meal, feed
Nosh   food

Nosh up   1. very big meal; 2. to eat
Nosey parker   stickybeak
Not a bad old stick   a good person
Not bad   good, excellent
Not for quids   no way
Not much chop   not good, below standards
Not on your Nellie   no way
Not the full quid   insane, stupid
Nothing between the ears   a foolish or stupid person
Nous   common sense
Nozzle   the nose
Nuddy   in the nude
Nugget   a stocky thickset person
Nuggety   a stocky thickset person, solidly built
Nulla-nulla   an aboriginal club, weapon
Numb skull   fool, idiot
Numbnuts   ineffectual man
Numbskull   dim-witted person, fool, idiot
Nut   1. head; 2. eccentric or insane person; 3. enthusiast; 4. testicle
Nut case   1. eccentric person; 2. crazy person
Nut chokers   mens' underwear, briefs, underpants
Nut house   an asylum
Nut out   work out, solve a problem
Nutted   castrated
Nympho   a nymphomaniac
O.P.   overproof as in rum
O.S.   overseas
Oath!   definitely; yes!
Obs   objections
Ocean-going   any seaworthy vessel

Ocker   1. stereotypical uncultured Australian; 2. destinctively Australian
Ockerism   referring to the ocker character
Odd jobs   casual work
Off colour   sick, unwell
Off like a bride's nightie   1. quickly remove clothing; 2. departed quickly
Off like a rocket   1. successful event; 2. depart quickly
Offsider   1. an assistant; 2. partner
Oi   hey you
Oinker   a pig
Okey dokey   things are good, okay
Old biddy   an old women
Old bomb   a dilapidated vehicle
Old codger   an old man
Old coot   an old person
Old fella   penis
Old flame   a lover from the past
Old fogey   an old-fashioned person

Greg spent all day **on the blower** trying to track down the **old codger** who left his **jumper** on the bus.

Oldies   aged parents
On a bender   drinking to excess
On a sticky wicket   in trouble
On the blink   broken down, not working
On the blower   on the phone
On the bludge   cadging money
On the cuff   on credit
On the dole   receiving social security benefits whilst unemployed
On the grog   drinking alcohol in excess
On the house   free drinks
On the level   honest
On the nose   smelly
On ya   good on you, well done

On your bike   get out of here, go
On your Pat Malone   on your own, alone
One and all   everybody
One and only   unique
One-arm bandit   a poker machine
One for the road   last drink
One tonner   a small truck, utility
One-eyed trouser snake   a penis
Oodles   large quantities
Op   1. surgical operation; 2. operator
Op shop   opportunity shop selling second hand goods
Optic nerve   a perve
Out cold   unconscious
Out of it   1. incapacitated as a result of alcohol or drugs; 2. spaced out
Outback   inland Australia, sparsely settled
Outstation   remote from main homestead
Over the hill   getting old
Overland trout   a goanna, lizard
Overlander   one who droves stock over long distances
Ow   sudden pain
Own up   admit, confess
Ow-ya-goin?   how are you?
Oz   Australia, an Australian
Ozzie   an Australian person
PJ's   pyjamas
Pack death   to be very afraid, scared
Pack it in   to quit
Paddo   Paddington, a suburb in Sydney and Brisbane
Paddock   an area of land enclosed by a fence
Panties   woman's underpants

The **one arm bandit** was operated by a lever on the side but today's **pokies** are operated by buttons on the front panel.

Parson's nose   the tail of a cooked chicken
Party pooper   a person who spoils a party
Pash   a kiss and cuddle
Pass away   to die
Pass round the hat   take up a collection
Pass wind   to fart
Passion pit   a drive in cinema
Pat Malone   on your own, alone
Pav   a pavlova; sweet meringue dessert cake
Payback   retaliatory action taken according to tribal code by aborigines
Pea soup   a thick fog
Pearler   something very good
Pearlies   teeth
Pecking order   social standing
Pee   urinate
Peepers   eyes
Pegs   1. legs; 2. teeth
Perve   one person lustfully eyeing another person
Petrol head   a person obsessed by his or her car
Piccaninny   an aboriginal child, baby
Picker up   a person who picks up the shorn fleeces in the sheering shed
Piddle   to urinate
Piece of piss   quite simple
Pig rooting   a horse bucking
Pig's arse   highly unlikely
Piker   one who leaves early, pulls out of a situation
Pink slip, get the   get the sack, fired; lose one's job
Pinny   an apron
Pins   legs
Pint   large glass of beer mainly in South Australia

Piss 1. to urinate; 2. alcohol

Piss head drunkard

Piss off depart, leave

Piss pot an alcoholic, heavy drinker

Plate, bring a bring a plate of food to a party or barbeque

Plates of meat feet

Plodder a slow worker

Plonk very cheap wine

Pocket billiards hands in pockets and play with genitals

Pointing Percy at the porcelain to urinate

Pokies poker machines

Pollies politicians

Pommy a British subject

Pong a bad smell

Poofter a homosexual man

Port a suitcase

Postie a mail delivery person

Pot a ten ounce beer glass (Queensland and Victoria only)

Pozzy/Pozzie/Possie position

Prang a car crash, accident

Prawn shrimp

Preggers pregnant

Pre-loved second-hand, used

Prezzie a gift, present

Pubes pubic hair

Pull your head in mind your own business

Puffed out of breath, tired

Pug a boxer

Puka large extended stomach

Puke vomit

Aussie's love a **barbie** and a prawn on the barbie is **"the duck's guts"**.

Punch-up   a fight
Punter   a gambler; bets money on horse or dog races
Pushing up daisies   to be dead
Put down   to kill an animal
Put the hard word on   ask a favour, loan
Put the mockers on   to cause bad luck
Quack   1. a bad doctor; 2. unqualified
Quake Isles   New Zealand
Quart-pot   a billycan
Queen   a homosexual
Queer   a homosexual
Queer bird   strange person, odd
Quick as greased lightning   very quick
Quick march   hurry up
Quick quid   easy money
Quick snort   a hasty alcoholic drink
Quickie   a short sexual encounter
Quid, make a   earn a living
Quid, not the full   person with a low IQ
Quim   female genitalia
Quits   gives up easily
Quitter   to give up easily
Quoit   bum, anus
R & R   rest and recreation
RS   rat shit; feeling bad
RSL   Returned Services League
Rabbit food   green vegetables, lettuce etc.
Rabbit on   talk nonsense
Rack off   please leave
Rack up   amass

A **punch-up** followed the **barney** between Big Bruce and **queer bird Nigel**.

Radical   great, fantastic

Rafferty's rules   no rules at all

Rag   1. newspaper; 2. argue; 3. gossip; 4. handkerchief

Rage   party

Rage on   continue to party

Rager   a person who parties hard

Rain dance   a ceremony believed to cause rain

Raining cats and dogs   very heavy rain

Rank and file   general people

Rapt   overjoyed

Rare as rocking horse shit   uncommon

Rare as hen's teeth   vary rare

Rat shit   no good, bad, lousy

Ratbag   an unreliable person, fool

Ration bag   a calico bag used to carry food

Rattle the dags   get a move on, hurry up

Rattler   a railway train

Ratty   1. worn out; 2. mildly eccentric

Rave   1. big dance party; 2. type of dance music; 3. animated conversation

Raw prawn   behaved offensively

Ready to drop   very pregnant

Reckon   1. absolutely; 2. suppose

Red centre   the centre of Australia

Red Ned   cheap red wine

Red steer   a bushfire

Redback   1. a $20 note; 2. a small poisonous spider with a red back

Reefer   a marijuana cigarette

Ref   referee

Refadex   Queensland street directory

Reffo   refugee

Bert used to be **flat broke** until one day he discovered how to invest by reading the financial **rag**.

Rego   motor vehicle registration
Reject   socially unacceptable person
Rellies   relatives, relations, kin
Rep   representative
Retard   clumsy or awkward person
Rev   engine revolution
Richard Cranium   a dickhead
Ridgy-didge   1. truth, on the level; 2. original, genuine; 3. refrigerator
Right, that'd be   accepting bad news
Righty-o/Righto   yes, okay
Ringbark   to kill a tree by cutting the bark off around the trunk
Ringdinger   a two-stroke motorcycle
Ringer   1. fast sheep shearer; 2. person or thing that resembles another
Ring-in   substitute, deceive
Rip   a dangerous under-current at the beach
Rip into   begin rapidly, eagerly
Rip off   1. a poor deal, overpriced item; 2. knockoff
Rip snorter   fantastic, outstanding
Ripe   1. something gone off; 2. eager, keen; 3. drunk; 4. obscene
Ripper   great, good
Ripper, you little   exclamation of delight to good news
Rissole   1. round meat or fish patty; 2. nickname for an RSL club
Road train   a rig of two, three or four trucks drawn by a prime mover
Roadie   1. last drink; 2. drink you take when leaving a function
Rock along   travel to, go, visit
Rock on   1. come on; 2. continue
Rock up   to arrive or turn up
Rogues' gallery   police file collection of criminals' photographs
Roll a joint   roll a marijuana cigarette
Rollie   a cigarette that you roll

Rolling in it   very wealthy
Roo   a kangaroo
Roo bar   a bar fixed to a vehicle to protect it against hitting kangaroos
Root for   cheer for, encourage
Root rat   one who is always looking for sex
Rooted   1. totally exhausted; 2. broken beyond repair; 3. abuse; go away!
Ropeable   very angry
Rort   a fraud
Rotten   drunk
Rouse   lose one's temper, chastise
Rub it in   remind one of their mistakes and failures
Rubbish   1. criticise; 2. garbage, trash; 3. tease
Ruckus   a commotion
Rugrat   ankle biter, small child
Rug up   dress warmly
Run on the smell of an oily rag   a car running on very little fuel
Runabout   a small motor boat
Runs   diarrhoea
Runt   1. a small person; 2. smallest in the litter
Rush   1. strong feeling of exhilaration and pleasure; 2. very busy
Saltie   a salt water crocodile
Salvo   a member of the Salvation Army
Sammie   a sandwich
Sandgroper   a person from Western Australia
Sandshoe   jogger, sneaker, trainer
Sanga/Sanger   sandwich

Good old fashioned toasted cheese **sanga**.

Sav   a saveloy; a type of sausage
Savvy   1. understand; 2. know; 3. intelligence; 4. commonsense
Scab   1. strike breaker; 2. stingy person; 3. bludge from someone
Scallywag   mischievious person, rascal

Scalper   one who buys function tickets and then sells them at a higher price

Scaly   a crocodile

Schooner   15 ounce glass of beer (Australia wide except South Australia)

Scone   1. the head; 2. a light cake or biscuit

Scoob   a marijuana cigarette, reefer

Scorcher   a very hot day

Scrag   unattractive woman

Scratchie   instant lottery ticket

Screamer   one who gets drunk on very little alcohol

Scrounge   to borrow or collect something

Scrub   bushland

Scrub up well   1. to be well dressed; 2. look good

Scrubbers   1. wild cattle; 2. unattractive woman

See ya   goodbye, see you later

Seedy   feeling sick; especially after a drinking spree

Semi   a large truck

Send her down Huey   send down the rain

Servo   a service station

Shack   a simple house

Shades   sunglasses

Shag on a rock, stands out like a   very obvious

Shaggy dog story   a very long story or joke with a pointless ending

Shanghai   1. sling-shot; 2. involve one in an activity against their wishes

Shanty   a small bush hotel

Shark bait   a swimmer in shark infested waters

Shark biscuit   one who is new to surfing

She'll be right   everything will be okay

Sheila   a young woman

Shindig   a lively party

Shit house   1. poor quality; 2. toilet

Shonky   poor quality goods

Shoot through   leave unexpectedly

Shout   buy a round of drinks

Shove off   go away, scat

Show pony   one who is concerned with appearances

Sick   1. totally excellent, cool; 2. disgusting, revolting

Sickie   take a day off sick from work

Sicko   disgusting revolting person, depraved

Silly duffer   a silly person

Silvertail   upper crust, social climber

Singlet   tank top, vest

Siphon the python   to urinate

Skeeter   a mosquito

Skidmark   mark of faeces on underwear

Skids   brakes

Skin and blister   sister

Skin flint   miser

Skinny dipping   nude swimming

Skite   to boast or brag

Skol   drink alcohol in one gulp

Sky pilot   a clergyman, priest

Sky rocket   pocket

Slab   a 24 pack of beer

Slab hut   a bush dwelling constructed from timber slabs

Slammer   prison

Slash   to urinate

Sleepout   a porch or verandah converted to a bedroom

Slice of the cake   a share in the profits

Sling   1. a bribe; 2. tip

Slog   hard work

Bob did time in the **slammer** for **knocking off** a **one tonner** and driving it through the front window of the **milk bar**.

Sloshed   very intoxicated
Slouch hat   Australian Army hat
Sly grog   alcohol sold by an unlicensed vendor
Smoko   smoke, tea or coffee break
Snags   sausages
Snake's hiss   to urinate, piss
Snakey   bad-tempered, irritable
Snooze   sleep, doze, nap
Snorker   a sausage
Snow/Snowy   a person with white or blonde hair
Snug as a bug in a rug   cosy
So long   goodbye
Sook   a weak timid person, a cry baby
Southpaw   left-handed person
Sozzled   intoxicated
Sparky   an electrician
Sparrow fart   dawn

Aussie's love to throw a few **snags** on the **barbie.**

Spat   minor argument, fight
Specs   glasses, spectacles
Spell   to have a rest
Spew   1. to vomit; 2. very angry; 3. disappointed at something
Spewin'   very angry, upset
Spiffy   excellent, great
Spin out   1. greatly amazed; 2. a vehicle skids and spins off the road
Spit the dummy   upset
Spruiker   a person who forcefully addresses prospective customers
Sprung   caught doing wrong
Spud   a potato
Spunky   attractive sexy person
Squib   a coward

Squirt   1. insignificant; 2. short person; 3. little child; 4. male urination

Squizz   to look

Starkers   1. totally naked; 2. insane

Station   homestead, ranch

Stayer   an animal (horse) or person of great endurance

Stick-up   a robbery at gun point

Stickybeak   a nosey person

Stirrer   one who causes trouble

Stock route   a track or road used by a drover

Stockman   a person who looks after livestock on a large farming property

Stoked   to be very happy

Stone-broke   no money

Stoned   drunk, intoxicated or under the influence of drugs

Stonkered   1. defeated; 2. drunk; 3. exhausted; 4. incapacitated

Storm stick   umbrella

Stoush   a brawl or fight

Straddie   North and South Stradbroke Island; near Brisbane, Queensland

Strapped for cash   short of money

Strewth   1. exclamation of surprise; 2. exclamation of irritation

Strides   trousers or pants

Strine   Australian slang

Stroppy   in a bad temper

Stubbies   men's work shorts

Stubby   a small bottle of beer

Stubby cooler   insulation casing for a stubby

Stuck-up   haughty, conceited

Stud   a male who considers himself extremely sexually attractive

Stuff   1. personal belongings; 2. render useless, ruin

Stuff it!   exclamation of frustration or anger

Stuffed   1. tired; 2. worn out; 3. broken; 4. full of food

Stuffed, I'll be expression of surprise
Stunned mullet dazed
Stunner thing or person of striking beauty
Subbie a sub-contractor
Suck face French kiss
Sunbake sunbathe
Sunnies sunglasses
Sunshine State Queensland
Super 1. personal retirement fund; 2. leaded petrol; 3. very good, great
Surfie person devoted to surfing, surfboard riding
Swag a roll of blankets
Swagman/Swaggie a tramp
Swansong a last performance
Sweet tooth liking sweet foods, lollies etc
Swipe steal
Sydneysider a person who lives in Sydney
TB tuberculosis
TLC tender loving care
Ta Thank you
Tacho tachometer
Tad little bit
Taddie tadpole
Tag to follow closely
Tag along join in with others
Tail 1. buttocks; 2. follow close behind
Tail throwing pulling a beast down by the tail
Tailgate drive very close to the vehicle in front
Take a gander have a look
Take a sickie take a work sick day when you're not sick
Take a squizz have a look

The number one thing on a **surfie's** mind is catching a **bonzer** wave.

Take-away   take-out food

Take some pickies/piccies   take photographs

Tall poppie   an important, successful person

Tall poppie syndrome   to criticise important, successful people

Tallie   750ml bottle of beer

Tally   counting

Tangle foot   one who's clumsy on his feet

Tanked   intoxicated, drunk

Tarp   a tarpaulin

Tart   an immoral woman, prostitute

Tassie   Tasmania

Taswegian   a person from Tasmania

Tat   a tattoo

Tea   evening meal

Ben **tucked** into his **take-away** the minute he arrived home.

Tear into   attack physically or verbally

Tear strips off   admonish severely

Tear-arse   a wild reckless person, fast driver

Tear-jerker   something very sad

Tech   Technical college

Techie   technician

Technicolour yawn   to vomit

Tee up   to organise a meeting

Tellie   television

Territorian   a person from the Northern Territory

The axe   to be dismissed, sacked

The big A   axed; get the sack, dismissed

The big C   cancer

The big spit   to vomit

The box   television

The Cross   Kings Cross, Sydney

The Don Sir Donald Bradman; the best ever batsman

The finger offensive gesture made by holding up the middle finger

The missus wife

The Rock Uluru, Ayers Rock

The sticks 1. in the country; 2. goal posts in a game of rugby or AFL

The Territory The Northern Territory

Thick dopey, fool

Thick-skinned one who does not like criticism or verbal abuse

Thin on top going bald

Thingo could be anything

This arvo this afternoon

Thongs cheap rubber backless sandals, flip-flops

Throw down a small bottle of beer that can be drunk quickly

Thunder box a toilet, dunny

Tick 1. credit; 2. moment or instant; 3. check mark

Ticker the heart

Tickets on yourself to have a high opinion of yourself

Tickle the ivories play the piano

Tickle the Peter to steal minor amounts from a till or cash register

Tiddly slightly drunk, tipsy

Tide's out beer glass needs topping up

Tie the knot to wed

Tiff an argument or a spat

Tiger country rough bushland

Tight 1. unwilling to spend; 2. close; nearly even

Tight as a fish's arse a very miserly person

Tim Tam chocolate sandwich biscuit coated in chocolate

Tin arsed a very lucky person

Tinned dog canned meat, camp pie

Tinnie 1. a can of beer; 2. a small aluminium boat; 3. lucky

Tip   1. offer a racing tip to someone; 2. rubbish dump

Tipsy   slightly drunk

Tit   female breast

Tit for tat   a hat

Toey   1. nervous, apprehensive; 2. keen, ready to go

Togs   a bathing suit, clothes

Tomahawk   a small axe

Too right   definitely

Top drop   a good bottle of wine or a good beer

Top end   northern part of the Northern Territory

Tosser   annoying person, jerk

Trackie daks   tracksuit pants

Trackies   track suit

Troppo   gone mad, insane

Trots   1. having diarrhoea; 2. harness horse racing

Truckie   a truck driver

True blue   1. genuine; 2. a loyal person

Tuck in   to eat, have a meal

Tucker   food

Tucker bag   a food carrying bag

Turps   1. alcoholic drink; 2. turpentine

Turps, hit the   a drinking binge

Tweeds   trousers, pants

The **trots** is a horse race focusing on the horse's gait and requires the horse to pull a two-wheeled cart called a sulky.

Twinkle toes   a good dancer

Twit   a dull, stupid person

Two-pot screamer   a very cheap drunk

Two-up   a gambling game with two coins, heads or tails

Tyke   a Roman Catholic

U-ee   a U turn on the road

Ugg boots/Uggies   boots made of sheepskin

Ugly as sin   a very ugly person
Umpie   umpire
Umpteen   many, large amount
Unco   awkward, clumsy person
Under the weather   1. feeling poorly; 2. hungover
Underdaks   underpants
Underdog   a team or organisation not expected to win
Undies   underpants
Uni   university
Unit   a flat or apartment
Unreal!   excellent!
Unsung hero   a person who is not celebrated or recognised
Unwind   to relax, take it easy
Up a gum tree   in difficulties
Up and about   active after an illness or sleep
Up at sparrow fart   rising very early
Up oneself   have a high opinion of oneself
Up somebody, to get   to berate somebody
Up the creek in a barbed wire canoe without a paddle   bad situation
Up the duff   pregnant
Up to putty   no good, worthless
Urger   a racecourse tipster
Useful as tits on a bull   1. incompetent person; 2. useless person or thing
User   1. one who exploits other people; 2. drug addict
Ute   a utility; open-backed work vehicle
VB   Victoria bitter, a popular Australian beer
Vacuum   a vacuum cleaner
Valley, the   Fortitude Valley, Brisbane
Vamoose   depart quickly
Vee-dub   a Volkswagen car

Veg out   relax

Vegemite   a dark-brown savoury sandwich spread made from yeast extract

Veggies   vegetables

Vego   a vegetarian

Verbal diarrhoea   constant talking

Vet   1. Veterinary surgeon; 2. a war veteran

Vibe   1. atmosphere; 2. feeling; 3. rhythm; 4. signals sent out to someone

Vinnie's   St Vincent de Paul charity shop

Vino   wine

Vocal   vocabulary

WACA   1. Western Australian Cricket Association; 2. Perth cricket ground

Wacked   1. exhausted; 2. out of it

Waddie   a baton or club

Wadjamacallit   something you don't know the name of

Waffle   talking nonsense

Wag   1. an amusing person, a joker; 2. skip school, truancy

Walkabout   1. gone missing; 2. an extended trip or tour on foot

Wallop   thrash, punch with force

Walloper   a policeman

Wally   1. a stupid person; 2. wallet

Waltzing Matilda   1. carry one's swag; 2. well known Australian song

Wanker   1. a stupid person; 2. an arrogant person; 3. an amusing person

Wanna   want to

Wanna-be   one who tries very hard without success

Washer   a face towel

Wasted   1. exhausted; 2. under the effects of alcohol or drugs

Water bag   a portable water container

Water the horse   to urinate

Watering hole   one's favourite pub or hotel

Way   extremely

Weaner   a calf no longer feeding from its mother
Wedding tackle   a male's sexual organs
Wedgie   prank where one's pants are grabbed and pulled up sharply
Wee   urine, to urinate
Weekend warrior   person in the army reserve
Weekender   holiday house
Weenies   small frankfurts
Well-heeled   a wealthy person
Well-to-do   rich, prosperous
Wellies   Wellington boots or gumboots
Wet, the   rainy season in Northern Australia from December to March
Wettie   a wetsuit
Whacked   drunk, intoxicated
Whaler   a bush nomad
Wharfie   a dock worker
What's the damage?   how much does it cost?
Whatsaname   used when unable to recall real name of person or thing
When the eagle shits   pay day
Whew   expressing relief
Whiffie   offensive smell
Whinge   to whimper, complain
Whip around   collect money
Whipped   defeated
White pointers   topless female sunbathers or bathers
Whirlybird   a helicopter
White ant   to go behind someone's back
White leghorn   a female lawn bowler
Whoop whoop   a long way away
Whose shout?   whose turn to buy the drinks?
Wifey   your wife or spouse

Wig warmer a hat

Willie a penis

Willy willy a brief dust storm of cyclonic nature

Wimp a weak person

Windies West Indian cricket team

Wing-ding a big party

Wino alcoholic, addicted to wine

Winkers the eyes

Witchety grub a large white grub found in wood

Wizz to urinate

Wobbly losing your temper

Wog 1. flu or a cold; 2. annoying insect; 3. person of Mediterranean origin

Wombat one who eats, roots and leaves

Wonky 1. unstable, unsteady; 2. poor condition

Wooden spoon a prize for coming last

Woofer a dog

Woofter a homosexual man

Woolshed a shed where sheep are shorn

Woop woop 1. middle of nowhere; 2. small insignificant town

Wouldn't be dead for quids to be alive and well

Wouldn't piss on you if you were on fire expression of utter contempt

Wouldn't work in an iron lung a very lazy person

Wowser 1. a non drinker; 2. a puritan

Wrung-out exhausted, tired-out

Wuss timid person, coward

XXXX Queensland Four X Beer

Ya you, your

Yabber talk a lot, chat

Yabbie/Yabby Australian freshwater crayfish

Yack 1. talk a lot; 2. chat; 3. vomit

The freshwater **yabby** is often caught for food.

Yachtie   a person who sails on yachts
Yacker/Yakka/Yakker   hard work
Yahoo   1. a reckless person, lout, uncouth; 2. exclamation of delight
Yair/Yeah   yes
Yank   1. an American; 2. to tell a lie
Yank tank   large American manufactured car
Yap   talk continuously
Yarn   1. a story; 2. talking with somebody
Yikes   mild exclamation of concern
Yobbo   a rude person, lout, hooligan
Yodel   to vomit
Yonks   a long period of time
You beaut/beauty   something good
You wish   an expression referring to one with unrealistic expectations
Young'un   a youngster
You're not wrong   you are right
Youse   plural for you
Yowie   mythical monster
Yuck   expression of disgust, unpleasant
Yuppie   young urban professional person with a high disposable income
Z grade   the lowest quality
Zac/Zack   old currency (sixpence) now five cents
Zap   1. cook in the microwave; 2. annihilate; 3. electric shock; 4. exhausted
Zebra crossing   a pedestrian crossing with broad white painted lines
Zeds   sleep, snooze
Ziff   unshaven, beard
Zilch   nil, nothing
Zip   zero, nothing
Zit   acne, pimples
Zonked   1. very tired; 2. drunk

Notes